A COUNTRY FOR

and

MY CANADIAN UNCLE

Also by Iain Crichton Smith from Carcanet

The Human Face
The Leaf and the Marble
Selected Poems
Collected Poems

Iain Crichton Smith

A COUNTRY FOR OLD MEN
and
MY CANADIAN UNCLE

CARCANET

First published in 2000 by
Carcanet Press Limited
4th Floor, Conavon Court
12-16 Blackfriars Street
Manchester M3 5BQ

A CIP catalogue record for this book
is available from the British Library
ISBN 1 85754 474 9

The publisher acknowledges financial assistance
from the Arts Council of England

Set in 10pt Bembo by Bryan Williamson, Frome
Printed and bound in England by SRP Ltd, Exeter

Contents

A COUNTRY FOR OLD MEN

A COUNTRY FOR OLD MEN

The Old Man

The old man does not think of himself as old
even when he sees children playing around the rowan tree

and around the garden well which has little water in it
though skin flakes from his stony head which he imagines as Roman

especially when he visits Italy and the peninsula of Sirmio.
Nevertheless, the old man has nightmares

of the friends he betrayed and who are now in Hades
at a smoky cocktail party vigorously talking.

He dreams of his clumsiness and inabilities
as he stands trembling before a spectral teacher

and a blackboard scribbled with incomprehensible words.
The dead extend their hands from hospital beds.

Who are these people racing towards him in his dream
passing milestone after milestone in their white dresses,

and who is driving calmly towards his destiny?
The old man without faith scratches his head

and hopes to let the bathwater cleanse him
and be perfumed by talc, shaving cream and soap.

But he knows that he is an arrangement of bones
and of flaking skin which hangs about him like a tent.

He remembers with anguish his adolescent over-confidence
and his cruelty to those who could not answer.

He remembers the moon shining over a loved city
and his boots echoing over its cobbles.

He remembers the drifters and motor boats he drew on rainy days
and the leaking toilets of his primary school.

He remembers his own invincible egotism
clearer to him than anything he reads

or the buzzard on the fence post or the trembling mouse.
All these he remembers, the old man who wishes to be loved,

whose stone head hangs out among temporary washing
and who watches his own nocturnal plays without dénouement.

Those Who Talk to the Wind

Those who talk to the wind
in their jesters' tunics
what shall be said of them?

Those who have grown tired
of the ambiguities,
the ironies, the hypocrisies.
the double colours,
what shall be said of them?

Let them go to islands
and speak to the stones
which do not change
and also to the wind
which is severe with daffodils.

I see them,
yes, I see them,
in the many-coloured
jesters' tunics.
They are asking the wind
to cleanse them
and to blow through them
and through the mixter-maxter ideas
that protect them from the earth.

They are asking
to stand up like bridegrooms
with a new ring on their finger
and new music
to ruffle the bride's dress.

A new wind
a new rhythm
blowing over the moor
towards the old cottage
with the scarred door.

A new wind
a new rhythm
a new jester
dancing on the black hearse
with his new colours
and his intent white face
which is a mask for his joy.

Autumn

Autumn reminds one
of heavy wardrobes,
large and mahogany,
and of coalsheds
with frosty locks on them.

It reminds one
of tenements
with broken windows
and dogs running through puddles
to windy appointments.

It reminds one
of postmen
humping their bags
over fences and ditches
towards a spectral house.

It reminds one
of Charity Shops
with suits and shirts,
blouses and skirts,
and books from dimmed authors.

It reminds one
of those who have left
to seek new countries
and who gaze into glasses
thinking of the old one.

In autumn
children play with a coloured ball
beside the sea
where the sand rises behind them
in a fragile statue.

Shorts

FAME

I tell you that fame
is just a disease.
Better eat cheese
and bread in the sun

than look in the news
for your own great name
or stare in the mirror
to transform you, if lame.

MURDO'S GREETING

Glad to see you, says Murdo,
even though he means
I'll smash you to smithereens
in spite of your hair-do.

Come again, says Murdo.
A kick up the bum
would be a blow for the artist
against the humdrum.

POETS

Virgil and Lucretius
are to me more precious
than multifarious Tescos
with its baskets of wire.

ROMAN

How stylish modern Romans are. But
in past centuries they shut

gladiators in with proud
lions to entertain the crowd.

LOVE

Amor vincit omnia, says
the poet with his lavish praise.

But what of Alzheimers, Murdo asks
in his final mask of masks.

KEATS

Beauty is truth, truth beauty, Keats said
lying on his consumptive marble bed.

AFTERWARDS

Metaphysics, what a bore.
There's really nothing beyond that door.

B AND B

The B and B signs swing high –
here's a spider, there's a fly.

FATTY

Says this fat chip-eating and true-blue
lager-swilling lout. It's effing true

Papists and darkies are all effing dumb.

Michelangelo, Gandhi – and then him!

The Secret Sorrow

Yes, the leaves are turning brown,
the year's at the turn,
and I am listening to some secret sorrow
inside my heart.

A secret frosty sorrow
is chilling my typewriter
and my pen
is slowly becoming an icicle.

Why is this? Tell me
the reason for this melancholy
and my thoughts of the Middle Ages
where there were many skeletons

and red crosses on houses
and Death striding briskly about
with a long moon-shaped scythe.

Could I gather the brown leaves
and put them together in a book
and publish them?

Would they break the heart
of an editor
sitting in a green chair
staring out of the window,
his brown cigar waxing and waning?

Names

In the cemetery at Aignish
the first name I see is Christina Campbell,
the name of my own mother
though she is not buried here.

And the names of many youths
lost at sea
on ships like the *Rawalpindi*
or the *Iolaire*.

The sea before me is glittering
and ducks flying over
a white avenue of light.

This is a township by the sea
where the villagers gather together
in eternal harmony
and the waves of green earth
are everlastingly fixed.

Look, an astonishing sight.
Here is a 'Charles Dickens'
surely an incomer
among the Macleods.

Dear novelist I read you intensely
when I was a sick child
your orphan Oliver
holding out his bare plate.

And here is your namesake
lying in Aignish
and his tall marble page
standing solidly against the wind.

Shorts

DRAMA WORKSHOP

This is what I tell them about drama.
A stranger comes to the door
and the arranged plates fall off the walls.

VISIT

This is the primary school I attended.
There are bright drawings on the walls
but no fierce streaming toilet rain.

FENCES

There seem to be more fences
which however do not keep the wind out
nor the rays of the setting sun.

GRASS

The grass streams all one way
but there is no dénouement
to which it points.

My Village

My village seems to be sleeping quietly –
no one to be seen
on its one long street.

No one hanging out washing
or digging in the fields
or moving cows or sheep
or hammering on posts.

Children, where are you?
Why are you not chasing the cloud shadows
or the seagulls
or throwing stones at telegraph poles?

Such calm, such calm.
I can hear the sound of the sea
as it slides over the sand.

Its whooshing sigh
as of interminable boredom
among the green rockpools
with their scuttling crabs.

Street of houses
show me you are alive,
you impatient children,

chase each other over the moor
of purple blueberries
towards the blue wall of the horizon.

Shorts

THE THEATRE

The lights come up on the stage.
It is magic.
It is our own translated world.

THE ACTRESS

Here you are in this shop.
Last night you had blue light
nibbling at your long marble gown.

RAIN

Rain falls outside the theatre
and hail and snow and wind.
There's also that black snail with two horns.

THE STRANGER

Someone is hammering on the door.
It is the black stranger
bearing turbulence.

HALLOWEEN (1)

They stood in silence
then removed their masks.
And below each mask there was another one.

HALLOWEEN (2)

Give them these apples from the apple tree.
In autumn they are wrinkled as their faces
but pink and round below the clayey masks.

HALLOWEEN (3)

I see you, beasts of our zodiac.
The lion attacks the mild sheep.
But Dracula attacks the clumsy bear.

HALLOWEEN (4)

Night of mimic cruelty. Above
the stiff masks the round moon sails,
a plate that mirrors bestiality.

Ashes

I scatter my brother's ashes on the sand.

The tide is breathing gently in and out.

I remember you in short trousers
climbing the pier's iron stairs
while the bees hummed furiously in the grass.

Now you have died in Australia,
with its incomprehensible deserts.
You set off with such youthful hope.

So we come down to a handful of ash
by the brine nosing like a dog
and that is all there is of those years.

Your suit (instead of shorts in Australia)
steadily burning like a last sunset,
a final fire among the local crofts.

Old Lady

I salute this gallant old lady
as I might a Roman heroine.

Protected by her Shakespeare
and her lovely classics
and her memories of a girls' school
she faces age with style.

She switches on the light
in a lonely house.
Daily through the window
she watches the leaves fall.

And she has a quotation from Shakespeare
with which to encounter death.

She will wear her quotations like a cloak
when he knocks on the door
and stands on the threshold
with, behind him, the moon.

A cup of coffee, she asks him
in her cool controlled voice,
you must be quite cold.

Is it as you like it?
she says remembering the wind
which blows through the leaves
of that Shakespearean play.

And she shivers a little
but retains her dignity
to the very end,

sitting quite upright
as the scythe-shaped moon
shines over the pale wood.

Shorts

LIBRARY

As I give a reading
in the city library
I am surrounded by
Tolstoy and Dostoevsky.

Also by Virgil and Homer
and many others.
Tell me, towering eagles,
how you like my voice.

CHARITY SHOPS

Oxfam, Save the Children,
Sue Ryder, Cancer Research,
I buy your worn books
so that people may not be parched

without transparent water.
How wonderful to tell,
that one may read a book
as look in a new well.

THE RED VAN

The red van brings
our letters every day.
In summer how it sparkles
between tree and tree,

as if it was a blossom
with its letters made from leaves.
Our technical Mercury
flashing among new groves.

For A.J. and M.

You are leaving your house
and you do not wish to go
from the hills, the sea, the slow
walks to the World War statue.

This place where your children grew,
this variegated mirror

of all your past acts.
See how the birds flow

on their annual migration.
See how they return to your eaves,
the faithful lively swallows

and you'll be somewhere else
among other distant hills
and where there is no sea

trying slowly to gather
a new map around you
in that not quite right weather
in a yet unanchored house
with its many photographs.

Shorts

BUS

There is no sorrow
worse than the sorrow
of seeing the last bus
draw away from the kerb.

BOOKS

How many books has Catherine Cookson written
Or Simenon,
Or Creasey?

How many Emily Brontë?
One only
echoing from the heart and from stone.

THOUGHTS

Pull thoughts out of your head.
Pull fish out of the sea.

But there always falls
the shark's gliding shadow.

TRAGEDY

Suddenly a whole tragedy
can be born out of a handkerchief

white as a small receding sail.

CONVERSATION

Two men converse
in armchairs made of salt
in front of the brine
and its unconfined whispers.

HORSE

Lackadaisically
it stares down at the ground

with its wealth of unbridled daisies.

DEATH

Come in, tall skeleton,
ladder of bones,

fold yourself into a chair,
and have a small sherry.

Children

You are all preparing to go to school
as the sky becomes pink among clouds.

It is an air from the past
that I breathe here in this kitchen
as you stand about in your blacks and reds.

Would I return?
No I would not return
I would not retrace my steps
with my bag over my shoulder
over these marshy paths.

And the lark trilling in the sky
and the stones taking on shape
and the whistle from the school gates.

Forward, forward, you go
with your electronic maps,
backwards and backwards I go
to a zigzag of chalk

to a globe painted with red,
to a long blue register,
to a tall lady without fables
but with the accuracy of arithmetic.

I see you run over the horizon
to an incomprehensible future
with your unmythological sandals
gulping the raw morning air.

On a Photograph by Dan Morrison

Seven women in deep black
walk to the church service in Lewis

Lined up together
they look like heavy-set Russians
from an isolated valley

Does God prefer black
to the colour of the poetic rainbows
which are bridges over the moors
and the scarred peat banks?

Does he prefer light to be sunk
in these cheap furs and coats,
in this sturdy Politburo
arranged in a black row.

O let there be colour in your church
such as a stained glass window
hung up in the daylight
above the wind-driven grass.

Shorts

KIERKEGAARD

The Famous Dane Kierkegaard
was both philosopher and bard.
His tremendously glowing brain
was born of a disfigured body's pain.

AUTUMN

Darkness descends —
and the cold winds.
And the leaves make a whirling stir
in front of our green directional car.

THE SUN

The sun sinks to its grave —
but some time later like the brave
it rises with great glaring face
projecting itself through frosty space.

RAINBOW

Rainbow touching that sharp field
crayon of a happy child
bridging from there down to here
fading through the bones of deer.

PHEASANT IN A CEMETERY

Angels they say would land on ground,
but for me I love the grand
bridal pheasant, brilliant red,
among the annotated dead.

Memory

I remember the great footballers, Hoddan and Stoodie,
and the green pitch on which they used to play.

It was during the consumptive years of the forties
that they dribbled past opponent after opponent

in their red jerseys which shone as bright as blood.

They were our tall heroes under the blue
skies, while the goalkeeper leaped about in yellow gloves

in his netted cage on Goathill in the breeze.

O they dribbled past Death, with his thin ribs,
and they jumped high as the white clouds

and the ball was the globe on which our hopes turned.

Shorts

(1)

What a bore
to get up from one's chair
and go to dinner
with someone who talks lengthily about the or-
al tradition.

(2)

Or to watch a tiny girl
with hands on hips
make complicated twirls
on a sodden open-air stage.

(3)

Or listen to stories
about salmon or deer
told by big moustached Tories
red-faced as fire
by desolate water-logged quarries.

(4)

Or hear a man in a drooping kilt
sing forty seven verses —
as black as hearses —
of a melancholy dirge about seals.

(5)

Or hear a pious woman
with a drop at her nose
relate scandals in prose
of a purely Christian kind.

(6)

Or try to see
how a complicated family tree
works –
when one does not care
about aunt, uncle or grandmother
any more than Turks.

(7)

Or try to pull your elbow
from a sentimental fellow
who weeps about heather and thatch –
and wears a multi-gadget digital watch.

(8)

Or listen to the lies
of someone who 'told his boss off'
or instructed in the war
his 'totally useless commander'.

December

The lid of the frosted bin
leans like an islander's cap
at a rakish angle.

But the hills are triangles
on a white jotter
as in a classroom safe and calm.

First World War Soldier

You struggle through the mud towards us
till eventually you slow to stone.

Suddenly the gunfire ceases
and you stand there with smoky sockets

while the sculptor carves your name
above the mud and the poppies.

You stare blindly across the fields
to where the children are playing

and the brown cows are lying down.

Such a mob of summer flies

buzzing and hissing. And the water
distant as a mirror or a mirage.

O stand therefore my young soldier
whom the gunfire has fixed at eighteen

with a poppy blooming on your breast.

Stand there, you are so young
I shall read about you in books

and on walks I shall stop and watch you
leaning wearily on your rifle like a staff.

Shorts

HIGHLAND HOTEL

Huge room in the hotel – O how dire
Tremendous portraits, juke-box – but no fire.

RANNOCH MOOR

Rannoch Moor where Eliot starves for the rifle,
how they tower up these tall post-modernist deer.

MAN OF ACTION

Where is the poet who would not prefer
to be a pilot playing in blue air?

ICONS

Once they're icons they do nothing wrong
Even their idiocies, subjects for good song.

ART

When I was young the humming telephone wires
were targets for stones and no 'bare ruined choirs'.

IF

If I could cry
I don't think I would stop
forever.

CHILDREN

The children are walking eternally
towards ceaselessly unfolding graves.

AS AN ATHEIST

As an atheist
I would invite red boiling hell
for the murderers
of the green children.

CHILDREN

Children, you are willing to learn
everything we teach you.

On your obedient spectacles
falls a diseased Fascist light.

BOOKS

The books pile up in front of my window
so that I can hardly see out.

Gift

With our black bags of clothes for Bosnia
we do not as yet deserve extinction.

Our shadows of charity fall over the sniper
a little perhaps, a very little,

as he lines his sights onto a window,
onto a door, onto a blood-stained bridge.

Our black bags bounce across frontiers
to alleviate the nightmare of ruins

and the bitter ghosts of snowstorms.
Let the clothes in them stand up stiffly.

O do not shoot at them hate-filled sniper,
my brother by blood, by arm, by eye.

Let them stand up straight on the bridge.

New Year

The Old Year turns its rusty hinge
and the New Year steps out bright as a child

onto the floor of blue linoleum.
The redbreast is pecking at the bread

and the nuts lying on the frosty plate.
The child looks at it, then at the bullying crow

and learns its first lesson.
                              However,
it hears two doves cooing in the wood

and an uncontrollable joy seizes it
so that it dances barefoot on the floor
blue as the sky and quite reliable.

Later that night it sees intricate jewellery
winking at it companionably from space.

Old Folks' Party

They all wear paper crowns
at the Old Folks' Do,
these proper kings and queens
(and nobler than them too).

Some have wounds sharp and deep
and will switch the cold light on
to silent living rooms
with their unringing phones.

But at the moment they
boisterously sing
songs of an earlier day
in their late evening

though above the cakes and tea
you'll sometimes see a face
stare unprotectedly
as into widowing space.

The Doves

The doves are cooing in the woods.
The hammers have fallen silent.

My enemy has removed his florid face.

The leaves are growing quietly on the trees.
O see them,
the dewdrops like buttons on my jacket
which is grey like the doves' breasts.

In the Frost

In the frost the two sisters walk.
In the frost I hear them talk
of children, death, and common grief
and of the falling of the leaf.

In the white frost, in the white frost,
inside which ideas are lost
and we must be made of stone and mud
and the springlike brilliance of blood.

The Winter Mountains

Everywhere the white triangles of the snow
as if the local had become geometry
as if the deer had vanished into paper.

Triangles round us like real objects,
like Euclid's furniture staring out of the snow
in a polished glare as of intelligence

yet an alien stare also slightly bluish
with wilful shadows running over it
but no deer or flowers or leaves or stones.

As out of a book rises the white page
blatant, obvious, incurious,
whose shape will change though it does not know it yet.

In Winter

The two doves
eat from the frozen plate.
Always together,
their constant faithfulness
is a grey dress
which outlasts the enamel reds
and blues of pheasants.

Neighbour

Build me a bridge over the stream
to my neighbour's house
where he is standing in dungarees
in the fresh morning.

O ring of snowdrops
spread wherever you want
and you also blackbird
sing across the fences.

My neighbour, if the rain falls on you,
let it fall on me also
from the same black cloud
that does not recognise gates.

Bayble Bay

I look out towards Bayble Bay
with its small green island.
Water pours down the pane.
How we used to paint
drifters, trawlers, with smoky funnels
and butting prows.
                    The world
has diminished itself
to a bare cottage
where the draughty linoleum would lift
like a blue wave.
O Bayble Bay
the salt ignites
great staring vistas:
the sparkle of spring
displaces
long grey ridges.
I think really
the language of that sea
is Gaelic.
What else would it be
for us who learned English
after our knees had bowed
by its green rock-pools.

Morning in Taynuilt

The rasp of a saw
on a frosty morning,
a rook's caw,
a dove's cooing:

these would be yearned-for
in the killing fields
as smoke rises
in snaky folds

above the refugees
who leave loved trails
to stamp white roads
with their bloodied soles.

The Great Soldier

The great soldier retires to his farm
to grow roses and cabbages.

Suddenly a rider pulls up at the gate
shrouded with dust.

'They want you in order to save our country
our rivers, our pastures.'

And he rises from weeding, shading his eyes
against the red sun.

And he goes to cut down
the enemy in their efflorescent uniforms

slashing again and again with his sword
against their alien growth.

The Voice

The voice comes to me from deepest Ireland,
'I am safe, I am safe.'
It is midnight and the phone has just rung,
and the taxis are running to their termini
over the snake-blue lights.
'I am safe, I am safe,'
says the tiny voice with the rough accent
as of a stone climbing a hill forever.
There is eternal lightning among the churches,
a cross of green shining
to guide pedestrians over the abyss.
I am safe, safe, fixed forever in this minefield
of which my iron jacket is made,
of which my head is made and my heart is made.
The children fly through the skies like angels
with blood on their wings
and a man with broken knees stares in a pool
where he sees a rifle.
This is the Middle Ages again,
and the green leaves have blood on them
and Death with his scythe trots happily
up to what seems a safe ruby-coloured pane.

MacDiarmid

After the excitement in your head subsided
and you settled down in a landscape of grass and stone
you read your green Penguin detective stories.

The portrait of your flame-haired wife blazed above you
and dogs barked on the edge of the horizon
and planets shone in their aristocratic colours,

and the ghosts disappeared from thorn and thistle
and chimney smoke climbed straight into the air
and you lay on your white bed far from red Lenin.

Friends

After almost fifty years we meet again
who were once students together in Aberdeen.

Time has treated us with some violence.
Our voices seem to echo here in London's

vast environs with which you are *au fait*.
We were reared in Bayble, Lewis, near the bay's

monotonous resonance, then in Aberdeen
we were in post-war residence by a green

park: the cinemas our New World,
our smoky story books. And then we held

each to our different courses – you, Engineer,
I later chancy writer. For you to live

in London's colourful avenues seems so strange.
Once there were thatched houses then they changed

to white ones; and old buses strew the fields.
In Aberdeen the daffodil engilds

the vernal parks. Here I recall
famous streets and buildings from my well

of inexhaustible books. I know them all.

Now I shall go home and leave you here
by Strongbow Street or Archer Street.
                              Do you remember

Chapel Street and Summer Street? We are ghosts.
Past selves remain obstinately in the frosts

of Aberdeen or Lewis. Then we make new,
and these remain behind us, till we go through.

a gate as to the lounge or Duty Free.
And you are waving to me as I leave

this multitudinous city to fly north
with my fleshly albums of blurred photographs.

All Day

All day I have been reading.
I have lived inside books while the snow falls
very gently on the fields.
The mouse's small head is whitened
and the birds have a new weight on their wings.
I cannot stay inside this world forever.
Yesterday I saw an old man bowed in a chair
his face white with tedium and fear.
He was not able to read.
This was in a hospital
whose doors swung open and shut
faster than the pages of books.

The Village

Above the village the dark clouds mass and gather.
The gates are open but no one comes in,
though they are painted yellow as the sun.
All one can hear is silence everywhere,

apart from one man digging with a spade
who is patiently planting his gardenias.
Now and again he lifts his pale face
and the poised weight of his rough thistly head.

And no one passes along the empty road
except for a lumbering black dog, heavy-jawed.

Children

One storms at the piano, one plays the computer,
and one sits quietly reading literature

and the roads outside the door point different ways
towards their changing Scotlands, Europes, Asias.

Two Worlds

The grandchildren fish the Internet while I
remember how it was in summer, sweatily

to play with a fishing cork on a full-sized pitch
just slightly northward of my becalmed cottage.

The Old Men

On the dew on the faces of the young
and their hopefulness
the old men must not cast shadows.

For they remember how they would race
with a football along the wet grass
as if they were winged

and how spring leaves would touch the trams
as they set off in the morning
past devout cemeteries.

On the dew on the faces of the young
and their eyes which drink objects
and skies of early red mirrors

let the old men not cast shadows
or the knowledge of the depravities
which keep them at midnight awake.

Sincerity without Art

Sincerity without art
is not enduring.
Otherwise
would we not say
that 'In Memoriams'
are the summit of poetry.
'The heart'
what can 'the heart' say of itself
that is *aere perennis*.
Rather it should be cast in bronze
as on a Roman *via*
with a fountain
playing in the background
perhaps
In stylish Italy
where even the poorest
know how to dress
and the screams from open mouths
are rimmed in luminous gold.

Prague

Shall we go to Prague
far from home
where there are blazing windows
and tall spires
and aged cemeteries
where there are lively cafés
in which famous writers chatted
and a clock
where the apostles
walk in and out.
O those lovely bridges
and these stylish girls
and these vast cathedrals
how you fill the imagination
with your enduring art.
In a fresh breeze
let me stand forever
by the echoing Danube
gazing at the clock
in the moving stream.

To the Muse for Jon Silkin

For those who have served you
with such dedication
let there be a special place
where they can read forever
only the finest words

and hear the finest music
as the poet begins again
a fresh exploration
like a boat setting out
with unprecedented sails.

Interviewer

To ask me of my history,
to strip me of my mystery,

to talk about salt exile
or the hard Protestant will

or my attitude towards Nature
(who has never seen a vulture

a tiger or a lion
but a mauled rabbit dying)

or in your young tones
question me of tombstones

of my common ancestry
and whatever sky

they lived their lives beneath,
and my stories about Death

comically reeling
or potato peeling

in grey or scarlet coat.

O if only when you quote

you knew the real sweat
the real dust and debt

the real gale and ache
how you might forsake

a nervous shaking face
confronted by blank grass.

Europe

We travel in shadow
over the earth of Europe
in the twentieth century.
There are so many stains
on the local skies,
and the scars of fires,
and broken windows
in museums
and libraries.

The cemeteries too
are crowded with tombstones
left higgledy piggledy
among unmown grass:
and in old ghettoes
there are bright paintings
and cadaverous stars
composed by the children.

Europe, aged mother,
tired and wrinkled
I see you as an old
cailleach surviving
on terrifying fables
of rightful heirs blinded
by sizzling irons.

But I then also see you
as a young girl standing
with streaming blonde hair
in fine freshening April
at the prow of a boat
and the blue sails billowing
above the sharp brine
towards a new horizon.

Time to Stop

It is time to stop writing about the Highland Clearances etc.

'O welcome to you, blue cuckoo, with your melodious sweet song.'

The cuckoo does not know the Highland Clearances
nor does the lark.

Yet they live here and perch on the gravestones and sing.

It is time to stop writing about the Highland Clearances.

The scythe-beaked golden eagle catches the sun
and does not see watery portraits in the lochs.

The Old Woman

It took me a while to push her down,
the old woman dressed in black, into the graveyard
and listen to the music of the wind.

And learn to love the ripe corn and stubble
and the voice of the young man who sang all day
and the horizon which cut the sky like a knife.

And the rainbow too I learned to love,
that lovely bridge which arches our fences
and the scholarly owl perched among trees.

And avenues of trees, greenly shaded,
and stones, wood, leaves, all these I learned to love
and to hate the honey colour of coffins.

And old women telling black stories
as they swayed in their unconditional dreams.

Island, rise up and put on a fresh music.

Put on your comic, not your mournful song
about horses with heads like varnished fiddles
and the Callanish Stones swathed in pink and blue.

The Honoured One

'Ah,' the honoured one says, 'I did not deserve . . .'
And as he spoke the vulture's great curves

descended and fastened on his head.
Was I already dead? he asks. I must tread

warily among these bow-tied waiters,
these flowery compliments and windy structures,

the hot lens that zoom in on my bones
where once they bloomed spontaneously.
                                              Black-skirted crones

kneel at my sweet sad face, which sees for miles
past plates and glasses. The round sun smiles

above my bug-eyed cradle. And then, the rings
of these tremendous furious stinking wings.

The Wedding

The netted bride swoops about the room
in billowing white. The dancers meet and part.
O happy night, and sweet delirium.
Let nothing separate these two who start

among benevolence, music and red wine,
who gather later in the chancy ring
and wide companionship of Auld Lang Syne
and for this moment are a queen and king.

In the Garden

Pulling a tough root out of the soil
How stubborn is the power of the will.
It threw me backwards among thorns and stones
with its muscular flex as of earthy telephones.

Spring

Some poems should be hung out like advertisements
in blowy spring of yellow billowy tents

when Achilles returns to us, and all the Greeks,
and Hector walks among the bird-like beaks.

In Munster

Above old Munster the Anabaptists hung
strung below the steeples in the blue
with terrified eyes and parched tongue.
Who shall tell us what's untrue or true

when upside down on a fine market day
thirsting for apples and for oranges
your mouth become such swollen lumpy clay
who would be eagle in these challenges.

Parkhead

How is it that these splendid stadiums
are planted among grimy streets
where the shop windows are boarded
and black graffiti sign sad clouds?

How is it that these buoyant players
weave their patterns on a ground
which is surrounded by dark houses
which sniffle with a dampish wind?

These roars as of a lion
emit the repression of seven days:
and rage at inherited injustice
pours downwards towards the fresh grass.

And scarves are stretched taut by supporters
at the beginning of the game:
'We are with you, our dear champions,
though ourselves we cannot save.'

Then you walk from that arena
towards your crouched houses again
and the closes with misspelt slogans
and the roofs which let in the rain

jaunty after victory
or desperate because of loss
you with the most intense passions
hanging on the destiny of a cross

happy-go-lucky fanatics
who thirst for a magical move
in the midst of deceits and ruins
and wages which run away, like love.

It is Strange

It is 'exceeding strange'
to stand here for a photograph
with a rowan tree in front of me
and a mountain behind.

I am not used to these berries —
only to their wounds —
I am not used to such a mountain
and the deer straying on it.

I grew up on an island
of moors and daffodils
of red heather and larks
and scarred peatbanks.

I grew up by the sea
with its slow liners
etched in silver
on a fine plate.

Beautiful berries,
temporary wounds
which the weather will heal
and perpendicular mountain

I now grow used to you
as a new world opens
and the ambitious lark gives place
to the homely redbreast.

For A.J. Macleod
  (d. May 1998)

In the time of the winking leaves you died
who were as a brother to me through all seasons.
In winter you were armoured in endurance,
and in autumn you were not melancholy.
In spring you were hopeful and cheerful,
and now in summer you have declined to the earth,
ornate colourful and temporary.
At all times you were charitable.
The breeze blows your ashes where it will.
Of the good it can be said they left a fragrant name
which surrounds your perishable shape forever.

In Those Days

In those days that are called free
before I'd ever met you
my mind was a sky without motion
an ocean with fish that weren't mine
and so I was forgetful
or wholly innocent of the petty
chains that may suddenly writhe like snakes
in a world where each may claw the other
by the claw marks of his territory,
by his brutal and most lonely song,
his scent that hangs on barbed wire fences.
How peasant-like the airy princes
locking their dears in rings of scythes,
lidding their thrifty treasury,
their darlings whether gold or black
wintering in their granary.

Breughel

Your world is alive
with games and proverbs
with the vacant faces of the greedy,
with landscapes of ice.

What a multiplicity of beings
what a stubborn humanity
insisting on itself and without ideas!

Death and the devils
are as ordinary as potatoes
carried in a cart
through a fury of fire.

Death pokes with his lance
absently, with indifference.
Bodies are packed into carts
as if they were garbage.

Death clad in red
drives through the countryside
like an elegant spider
with his rustic prongs.

And you who are looking
carefully into the mirror
admiring your complexion,
remember Icarus

whose legs are disappearing
into the common water
white and unnoticed
by the farmer at the plough.

Art is how we solve
the problem of dying
in a country we paint
with flamboyant colours

till perhaps eventually
we will paint Him out of the picture
which hangs in an ordinary light
on a Dutch morning.

For Edwin Morgan

To swim out
into the impassioned light
and glint of the new,

as it seeks language
vulnerable, strange-spined,
blink-eyed

is for you mandatory.
Let the blue sky
bend over oddity

or even the monstrous –
The taste of poetry
is for you, this,

to substitute for the rose
in abandoned windows
the happy orphans.

Parting

She went away leaving us a letter
saying that 'Far from you I will love you better.'

What is it that has happened to her? She says
she feels constricted, must find her own way.

The birds in the colourful garden build their nests.
May is magnificently manifest

in azaleas, rhododendrons. Nature
repetitively creates its own future.

'What I am going to cannot be worse
than what I leave behind.'
                                        A curse

has settled on her. What did we do wrong?
F . . . off, she shouts, in a shrill alien tongue.

Let summer blaze, it will not burn away
crossed wires and errors. And who can now say

where the discontentment came from?
                                              Birds will try
their weak small wings against the towering sky

where new clouds settle, then create the dark.
She takes her starlike jewellery, swings her bag

with a jaunty confidence she does not feel.
Sparks of sharp anger haunt her parting heel.

The Seagulls

The seagulls still come to the door
of this country cottage, alighting with a whirr
and flap of their white wings, staring around
with their wild beaks, bringing a sea sound
to these tame roses. Their busy large
imperious bristling flourish
is not a disturbance but a reminder
of the briny water, and the beaked commander
of rock and wave, when in my youth I wavered
between tame and wild, my bleak gaze fixed homeward
from the sparking multitudes in which I played.

Blue

Into my sky-blue ash tray I tap my ash.
The sky is beautiful over the dead.

It has no thought, no rancour.
It is as perfectly unruffled as new carbon paper.

The earth is alive with broken music.
Dust blows along the roads.

And one schoolgirl races towards the next one,
almost a copy, but not quite.

Charity Shop

Save the Children, Oxfam, Cancer Research,
that is where the second-hand clothes are hung

in shadows, corners. And where are to be examined
shoes, belts, blouses, skirts, all the kind

largesse of others. Wear them, try them on.
Assume them as cloaks, aristocratic, Roman,

for these are history too. And sweat is seen
along that cuff, that sleeve, where the machine

shortened the arms. Terror from History comes,
as also roses, blood and leathery drums,

storms and large sorrows. But these clothes, hung
in silence here, inherited from the dying,

the live, the dead — wear them as statues do
their pride and passion, as if they were all new,

messages from your equals, who have trod
streets with these shoes or in that blouse flowered

vain and momentary. Out of the very graves
you walk, are changed.
                    Your breasts will tilt that blouse
towards a morning, fresh and garrulous.

At Night

To be so tired that the moon becomes a pillow
and that coloured images flash behind your closing eyes

and that the dead stand beside ditches when you flash past
in your car which is burning over the tarred road

and that the trees seem to be moving parallel to you
and you hear over and over the words of a favourite song

and you remember a man whom you knew in your forties
who at eighty is coping with a demented wife

and whose desperately tired face haunts you
like a face on a gravestone that is unable to sleep.

Such tiredness is not suitable for a man
whose ambitions were once as clear as posters.

It is hard to keep up with the moon. Let your head
lie once and for all on an amber-coloured cloud

except for the dependent network of people
that you drive towards dimly as into an urban web.

Old Woman

I see the old woman behind the flowering broom.
I have followed her from poem to poem

and her grey coat is almost hidden by that yellow and red
on a May day with white clouds overhead

billowing with pillows. Yes, she carries her bag
home from the village shop.
                          And behind her a stag

in my imagination rears its magnificent head
out of the stones and flowers and small hills of the dead.

Leaves

O you come towards me
you mirror-like twinklings of the leaves
you multiplicities

you numerousness, you shining millions,
you ample magniloquence
you solar riches

bouncing of your leaves like crystals
like marbles, like ballets,

like whatever is improvident

extravagant hilarious
the constant laughter of dew.

Poem for the Pamphlets of The International Festival of Poetry, London, 1998

She does not know that she has died
who has lived with him for sixty years.
Are you enjoying yourself, she says at the funeral
smiling brightly and dutifully.
Let the heart not burst, I say to myself,
let the fist not be shoved through the glass
though the blood could blossom like a rose.
You are getting bigger. I smaller,
she says with the same eager smile
wearing her white unstained gloves.

In the Attic

As if on scented winds, philosophy,
or days of knowledge in the attic, high
above the harvesters and fishermen,
or in the living grass or purple moors
the sun declining over the blue hills,
a red-hot griddle, or a blazing plate —
so they would come to me, all these characters
from their fresh pages, real novelties,
at least as genuine as the jerseyed ones
who swam among the crabs, and elegant
blue-suited herring in their echoing sea.

The Messenger

I think that the messenger will not appear,
for he has bad news.
Why should he come when he will be killed
though the bad news is not his fault?
If I were him I would hide in the thistles,
in ruined cottages and in caves.
The bad news is not his fault.
He did not direct the battle;
he did not accept the bribes,
he was not incompetent.
The soldiers lie with roses on their breasts.
The messenger was about to ride his horse:
instead he takes to the hills,
and hopes his name will be forgotten.
He will grow vegetables if they do not find him,
he will laze in the shadows in a wicker chair
if they do not cover him with earth,
the messenger whose fault it was not
but who could run faster than others towards his death.
No let the messenger escape
and let the bad news find its own way.

Not a Day for Dante

This is not a day for Dante to visit me
and come in at the yellow gate.
The sky is overcast as it is not in Italy,
the rain smoulders on the hills.
I do not think he will like the cold
and this village is much smaller than Florence.
I suppose he could pull his cloak about him
as he mutters his three-lined verses.
There is no one here to be consigned to hell
and its mountains of flame
there is none here to be stirred about with a trident.
No the sky is too lowering.
But if you want to read a book I have plenty
and certainly I would refer to you
as to the greatest of masters.

The Pond

The rabbit sits beside the pool
and the dove studies it.
It mirrors the sky and the clouds.
We will be happy to see frogs in it
and water lilies also.
I will take a chair and sit beside it
like a Chinese poet,
till the chair gradually becomes earthen
and a wagtail alights on my head
as if I weren't there.

Page after Page

We turn over page after page of the days.
Is it a tragedy or a comedy?
It is not, I think, either.
These colours simply dye the land.
These leaves twinkle and twinkle.
People pass on the road
and are finally swallowed by distance.

The Titanic

As the Titanic sinks
window after window is swallowed.
The men in evening suits topple over,
the captain looks down at his wet hands.
Icicles form on bracelets
and rings contract in the cold.
Never again will they be warm,
they would even accept a brazier
as the beggars in holed clothes do.
Such a huge disaster has befallen them,
their houses fall through the waves,
their maidservants and manservants,
their gleaming limousines.
They are trapped among glossy triangles
in a floating geometry of ice.
God, how did you let your diaries
cease at this point?
Who can offer a bribe to the sea.
How did our handbags fill with water?
How did the stars become so distant?
The night twinkles with ice.
None of us can walk on water.
My mouth is swallowing the brine
which swells all my pockets.

That House

That house is tall and narrow and stony
reminding me of Wuthering Heights
and Emily writing in a draughty room.
Such bony intensity was inhabiting
a place I think lacking in mirrors.
Outside the windows the larks sang
and the peewit called from the moor
and the sheep chewed the grass
and the sky was an ecclesiastic blue.
That house is so tall and eerie
standing up in a wide airy space
containing love, pain and ambition.
It is like a stone coffin placed upright
while on it the small birds perch
and listen to its music
and whose windows look out on infinity
and a high sky of consumptive red.

Joy

Joy such joy
as Wittgenstein said
on his death bed,

who would often say,
I'm so stupid today
and leave the lecture room

to go to Ireland
and the green wind
which didn't know language.

Such joy such joy
of the one who felt
the fierce stress
of struggling genius

and who was set
like a victim in
the engineered web
of an enchained
sentence.

Death has no meaning
in the language of the living.
Ungrieving you go into the dark
to that place
for which there is no language
but the grace
of dying like
the fall of an apple
on to unshadowed grass.

Synchronicity

How is it that when the steam rises from the kettle
that I think of the three witches in *Macbeth*
at the same time as there is a Gaelic song on the radio
about a broken-hearted widower sailing for Canada
where the snow will fall on a Hebridean grave
and the unshadowed fields of his early happiness.

On a Day

The green leaves twinkle in the sun and wind.
The red post-van stops at the yellow gate.
Is that winged Mercury descending from the doorway?
The moment is aflame with correspondences.
Tell me, tall girl walking your black dog
do you feel the clouds crowning your head?
Tell me, rabbit, do you look down the cat's red throat?
Or, linnet, tell me of the buzzard sitting in state.
There is no end to the revolutions of the wheel
and the shadows that replace each other.
Like cormorants we arise somewhere else
shaking the water from our wings, looking around us
at the bowed speculative heron reading the brine.

Ian Paisley

Ministerial demon, it would be nice if hellfire
(in which I do not believe) would have your crooked spire
poke like a trident in your poisonous mouth.
And that in your evening, dead children would seethe
about your blue bed, and snakes would breed
in the nightmarish videos of your neolithic creed.

For the Hebridean Celtic Festival

Listen, the isle's alive with noises
'full of sweet airs that give delight and hurt not'.
Let there be fiddle and accordion,
piano, clarsach and the mandolin,
the human voice, extravagant of its joys,
and not declamatory, imperious,
the gifts of music like a sparkling stream
in that bare rock and meagre living-room –
the overplus of life, the dance that spins
like the linked planets round our dazzling suns.

Paris

Paris, you are named after revolutionaries
and I recognise them all
from my safe history book.
I recognise a bath filling with blood
and the green coat of Robespierre
as he climbed the scaffold
clutching his red code.
There are clear vistas everywhere
in this designed city
to which Napoleon returned
with his genius and his spoils.
Here is the Seine
which winds through all that bloodshed,
and the vampirish aristocrats
who rise from their graves
to feed on peasants.
Cities of armies,
and of clear-headed writers
who abolished stained glass windows
Tramp tramp tramp go the legions
to Smolensk and Jena
and a tricorn hat
shadows whole countries.
Skeletons return from the war
and small boys beat drums
alongside old men
who have forgotten the slogans.
Listen, countless corpses are marching
with stiff white faces
though Hitler spared you
because they say he loved you.
Who is my neighbour
in this captive city
enchained and glowing?
Who is my neighbour
in this city of galleries
where paintings hang out in the wind
among the swastikas?

In this free city
the feet can go anywhere
especially to Montmartre
artistic and poor
where among slums
there are breezy easels.

City of blood,
and of paintings of angels,
I walk behind the *Grande Armée*
and the grey goosestep
and I see a stylish woman
standing pensively on a bridge
as if born from the Seine.

A Station Called Rome

There is a station called Rome on the Paris underground.

Drunkenly he climbed into the Holy City
with its languorous Tiber,

and its Roman imperial statues
and its air of ancient hauteur.

Strangely the language was what he was used to
and the stylish women similar

and the transparent fountains played
from their coats of green moss.

O let me see Nero
playing his bloodstained violin
in the grey Metro

and the bridge with faithful Horatius

and also the real Mona Lisa
with her fat secret smile.

Paris

The bridges of Paris hummed in the high wind.
The red cloud of Robespierre inflexibly burned

and the snaky Seine mirrored the tall
Grande Armée of Napoleon with its snow-white dull

whiskery faces, and its jigsaw limbs.
In this rational land there were no hymns

as Napoleon scribbles furiously with his pen
and the crystal Empire freezes in his brain.

Direct streets of reason. Doctor Guillotine
cuts very neatly along the dotted line

and heads roll like potatoes in the gutter.
Now buses nose towards the Eiffel Tower

and the Palace of Versailles lapped in green.

Systematic city, vistas shine

straightly down avenues. The bloody daughters
throw the Bastille open like morning shutters

and the beaked one watched from a stone wall
distant St Helena, watery and still.

At the Edinburgh Festival

Dressed like a Roman statue, and with white
dead-painted face, the motionless living man
stands like a senator in the Lawnmarket,

a ghost from some BC.
                          A coin is dropped
into his box and like some strange machine
his arms and head move slowly, as if new-shaped

by money. The spasm past,
it settles once again to ghostly Rome
cast on its dream among the cameras.

He Spoke

He spoke as if from the other side of death
quite clearly and quite impressively.

I think from your side it is tragedy
but from my side here it's really comedy
dry, not furious but temperate.

The tables spread with goodies for the guest
in blazing uniform looks aslant at best

and so does the orator with his spurious crown.
Young, the slightest shame is tragedy,

Old, it is comedy and cause for laughter
in a pure red weather in the evening.

MY CANADIAN UNCLE

My Canadian Uncle

1

Canada feels large and transient.
We leave Vancouver in a glittering sun,
heading for White Rock, my uncle's own
and carefully built house. We let the breeze
stream past us freshly through the open windows.
The traffic lights ahead of us hang down
at the road's centre, and we bullet on.
At 85 he's driving. He goes home
to Lewis every year, but all are dead
whom he once knew, all under white and red
flowers in the windy cemetery. He sits
crag-faced and tanned, short-sleeved, and beats the lights
with mischievous relish.

                                        Canada extends
from Vancouver northwards: to where once he saw
black bears chew berries on a calm cool day.
'Old son,' they told him at the station, 'You
may drive the month your visitors are here.
But after that . . .'

                                    'I'll tell you' (in the clear
air, he says), 'You can exceed the limit
by a mile or so.' We tremble in our seats.
Impossible Canada so vast and mild.
You're not a Lewisman, you're Canada's child.
He fires his long white Plymouth at the gate,
puts on his glasses, backs out of the light
into the garage, as if he steered a boat,
gets out and says, 'Well then this is it.'
The wooden house, the garden, and the snake
basking in sunlight on his own White Rock.

2

'A "cattle ship" it was, on which we sailed
in 1912, and in the Irish Sea

a storm blew up. The Hungarians were sick,
not used to oceans. (They grew up on land.)
Even the captain and crew were sick.
He came to us and said, "You know the sea.
You could rig a rope that would support their steps,
I mean the Europeans." So we did.
None of us Lewis boys, you see, was sick.
So we rigged a rope up and they walked by it,
those who could stand: the rest were in their berths.
And the captain told us, "Have some extra food
and nips of whisky" . . . So we said we would.

'Leaving the cookhouse then one night Hugh saw
a big white cake that stood on a wooden shelf.
"The First Class passengers, they cannot eat,
they're far too ill," he told us. And he smiled.
"We'll take it," and we did. We ate it all.
Though I didn't like the theft, I never said.
(Hugh is dead in Flanders years ago,
a merry fellow full of jokes and jests.)
The second night we saw a turkey. Hugh
hid it in his jacket and we threw
the bones to starboard in the pitch-black night.
"Where is my cake, my turkey?" said the cook.
"We never saw them," innocent Hugh replied.
I told him later he was just a crook,
and not to steal again. Neither he did.
The ship plunged on and the sky became raw red.
We were the only ones could drink or eat.
"You must have stomachs hard as iron plate,"
said the steward, born in Skye.

'There was a blacksmith
who'd sold his business, and sailed with us,
a muscular fellow who was always sick.
"The ship is sinking," Hugh called one day
and the blacksmith left his bunk and rushed on deck
to find it was another merry trick.
"I'll kill you," he stormed at Hugh. "Just you wait."
And Hugh laughed. Sure, I can see him yet
with his moustache in the cold greenish light.
And there was another man who lay in bed

104

clutching his Bible. We would bring him food,
he said he was so ill he couldn't move.
Then one fine morning, icy cold it was,
when our hands were burning if they touched cold steel,
someone shouted, "It is land at last."
(And there it was, Nova Scotia, like a ghost.)
And that man threw the Bible from him, rushed
up the companionway, he who'd been so ill.
He had mastered even Hugh with his wiles.
And Canada lay before us. We were young.
The First Class passengers climbed up on deck,
and the Hungarians and Germans too.
They stared astonished past that blinding blue
at Nova Scotia ghostly under snow.

'And so I remember John and James and Hugh
long dead in Flanders under poppies. The
ship was a cattle boat. But quite proudly we
landed in Canada in our salt-stained suits,
among that flurry of Canadian lights.
The streets were paved with gold, so it was said.
We rocked a little on that foreign tide
and then walked up the gangway to our lives.
Some to prosperity and some to graves.'

3

A woman was preaching in the church. He says:
In my young days it would not be possible.
She says: There is the credit and the loss,
the one written in black, the one in red.
She is pencil-thin, black skirted. Says, We'll sing
this hymn because I like it. And he smiles,
thinking of home and of the minister
who flared through hell, with bullock shoulders, with
a bullock chest and red infuriate eyes.
At the back of the church are information packs
on alcohol and grass. ('Grass,' he says,
thinking of meadows and of cemeteries.)
A woman preacher? How should she know the truth,
moon-tugged and pagan? Bearded fathers sat

105

in Lewis with their Bibles in their hands.
The sea that ran between us, feminine!

The masts pierce the black clouds. We enter the
uniform brilliance of Canada,
temporary, sparkling, superficial.
'God is a businessman. The black, the red.
Our lives are trades conducted in blind salt.'

4

Sitting in his garden in the sun
in my green Canadian jockey cap I dozed
below the cherries, colour of red wine.
The crows had pecked them to a rotten brown.
He had a wire strung out from the kitchen
which he would pull, to a clamour of loud cans,
which then would dance and dance and dance and dance.
A Stetson hat hung high above the garden.
He knew by sight each individual crow
so sleek and black, a devilish Free Church hue.
'Whatever we would get we would have to pay
for later. I once told a man –
from Paisley, I think he was, he was making fun
of Highlanders – I said to him one day,
"We had the best of food when I was young,
crowdie and salmon, oatcakes and fresh fish.
We lived like princes in so-called barren Lewis."'
I peered beneath the visor of my cap.
He stood beside the red and velvety rose
he'd planted for his wife. The shiny crows
were hovering round us. 'We never once
quarrelled, Mary and myself. And I composed
poems since she died. I said, No drugs.
I held her hand at the end. Here the graves
are flat, not upright. I will take you there.
Vandals steal the flowers.'

                                    Later he said
'I'll bring some girls I know along for tea.'
They were seventy years old and both had sticks.

We sat in the cherry garden in the fine
monotonous sunlight. The two ladies' hands
trembled among tea cups.

                              With a hose
he carefully watered the red Empire rose.

5

More than twenty channels on TV.
One day we watched a Nature programme.
A dog had met a porcupine on the road,
was trying to eat it, while each upright pin
needled his nose and eyes.

                         'You see that dog,
he'll not give up. But the porcupine will jag
him all day, if need be.'

                         Whose side did he take?
The porcupine's, the dog's? The sharp pins raked
the dog's fierce questing forehead.

                              Some had died
in Canada, in Flanders, for the road
was a hard dog's slog from Lewis to the snow.
(Such Douglas firs we saw! The world was stars
sparkling and brilliant as if at Christmas.)
The stray dog burrowed but the porcupine
defended stubbornly. The trenches spun
with flashes of bright fire.

                              It turned away
dejected, haggard, tail between its legs.
'That'll teach you,' said my uncle. *Nemo me
impune lacessit,'* sang the Scottish flag.
The Germans ghosted towards him in grey
with their thistly helmets, foggy, spiked, and rayed.
Icicles jagged moustached and stubborn Haig.

'My kidneys were infected in the war.
This major told me, You've got six months to live.
The pain disabled me. I lay in bed,
my back a trench that churned with fire and mud.
"So this is what you've come to after all,"
I told myself. The Canadian air felt chill.
I grieved and pitied my own piteous self.
I wrote to my sweetheart putting my marriage off
and lay and brooded. Then one day I rose
and played at handball till the sharp pain eased.
You haven't died a winter yet, I said,
gritting my teeth and mocking at the dead
who let themselves lie down in the cold grave
(as even in Lewis they would rise and moan
at a cold fire, and mumble of their faith,
the Bible a small tombstone in their hands).
So I was cured and later still I heard
that the Major who had warned me had since died.'

I smiled a little.

                                   'I've one kidney now
But I'm quite healthy.'

                                   No, he'd shouted, no,
to finite death. And here was I, a poet,
protected, nourished. His huge head burned bright
and rocky like a Lewis cliff. I knew
I would have died on the journey he had made
from war to war, from job to job. The dead
prospected among ores, delusive, poor.
I'd washed my soul out in pure literature
and listened, half in awe. The surly bear
munched at his berries in that northern air.
I munched at the berries of an old man's tales.
The sea boiled round a stray and salty sail.
The major died. My uncle shook his fist
at chewing death. A big white-hatted ghost
he towered and burned, and would not fail, not fail.

'I'll take you to see Smith,' he said one day.
'He's never been to church in Canada.
I'll tell you the cause of that. It was this way.
Before he embarked he met the minister.
(It might have been in 1902 or 3.)
The minister told him, I have heard them say
you worked in the Greenock shipyards on a Sunday.
You work on a Sunday yourself, young Smith replied,
and the minister wouldn't speak to him the day
he sailed for Canada. (He was just nineteen.)
What do you think of that? Of course you've been
an atheist from your youth, your mother said.
But God exists, you must remember that.
I'll meet my dearest Mary when I'm dead.
Each year I read the Bible, every word.
There's not a tribe whose name I can't recall.
I'm now at the Letters of the Apostle Paul.
I've got the Bible that my father had
with all our names in it. There is a God.
We go to another country, and we live.'
I listened while he argued with his friend,
who'd never been to church in Canada.
'It was an apple Eve and Adam ate.'
'No,' said Smith, 'it doesn't name the fruit.'
'It was an apple that in Paradise
the snake enticed them to,' my uncle said.

                                 And so they fought
over the apple or the nameless fruit.
'There is a God,' he said. 'You must have faith.
When I was young my mother punished me
for spilling milk on the floor. Did I tell you that?
"You mustn't spill the good fresh milk of God."
So she hung me in a creel above the fire.
By gosh, I felt the burning.'
                             And Smith said,

'Darwin proved that we all come from apes.'
'Garbage,' my uncle said. 'Have you ever seen
a graceless monkey change into a man.'
'But it's millions of years,' said Smith. 'Millions and more.'

'Garbage,' my uncle said. And Smith went on.
'What use is your appendix. Tell me that.
Darwin has proved that all of us have tails.'
'Tales,' said my uncle mockingly. 'I'd say
you're a bit of an ape yourself, but not me.'
'You're not a scientist,' Smith replied,
limping about the kitchen. For his pride
was punctured by my uncle's mocking laugh.
'These facts are proved.' But my uncle saw him off.
'You'll be saying next it was oranges or grapes
they had in Eden, that they were munched by apes.'
In great good humour he drove home that day.
'Of course he reads a lot but what he says
is garbage pure and simple.'

                                For his God
was large and merciless, violent, unflawed;
had guided him to Vancouver, from the doss-
houses of Winnipeg, and his gain and loss
were sure and evident. By each lonely grave
as far as the Arctic, God maintained his grave
and ceaseless watch, a munching ghost,
pensive and moony, and no soul was lost
but was herded from the dosshouses to fanks.
From crumby lodgings, oily, grease-embossed,
the unshaven tramps, itinerants, offered thanks,
bowed to the ground. 'O, I love you God
because you scourge me with your vicious rod.'

We sat in the garden among harmless snakes
in Canada, so sunny, without God,
and drank our coffee and ate scones and cake.

8

'I told you of the dosshouses,' he said.
'You had to wear your clothes in bed at night
or they'd be stolen by the morning. Sure.
Another thing. You'd look for any job,
even if you'd never done it. A rough carpenter
was what they offered me in Winnipeg.
Sure, I said, I'll take it.

            'I drove a sledge
once across a lake to get our food.
The overloaded sledge went through the ice.
I was floating in the water and my pipe
was floating with me. (It fell out of my mouth.)
Save yourself, they shouted from the bank:
but I was fumbling for my smoking pipe.
"Torquil loves his pipe more than his life,"
they laughed and shouted.

            'And another day
cutting a tree down in the month of May
I heard a machine gun stuttering in the wood.
I turned and crouched and peered. The hero stood
petrified in a forest by the Somme!
And all the time it was a woodpecker!
Imagine me, that fine heroic figure
frightened of a bird!

            'I was so young,
the world was there before me like a song,
and my tongue tasted it.

            'Another day
I was cutting trees and the snow fell down my neck
and melted there in spite of my big hat.
Dang this, I said, and threw the saw away,
handed my books in, and went off that day,
no work on the horizon, and my shirt
clinging to my back.

            'Some summer days
we'd strip right down, remove our pants and shirts,
and wash them in a stream as our mothers did.
The midges bit and bit and bit and bit.
Our pants were ribbons and our shirts the same.
There you are, Iain, you could write a poem,
only I can't ever rhyme your lines.
You cannot write like Service or like Burns.
Some nights I'd hang my shirt up on a nail
and it was frozen like a coat of mail.
I'd work knee deep in water. Why, I said,
did I ever leave my island?

111

'It was dead,
and adventure called me. That was the reason why.

'When I was young I went to Stornoway
I tied the horse up and walked down a street –
Point Street, I think it was – there was a fat
Recruiting Sergeant at the office door.
"How old are you?" he said. I said, "Sixteen."
"And would you like to join the army then?"
I said I was too young. "No, no," he said.
"You're tall enough." And measured me. "You'd pass
for eighteen any day." So I took the shilling
and told the postman, "I'm a soldier now.
If a letter comes, give it direct to me,
and not to my parents."

'So I ran away
with my melodeon in my case one day
and the first my parents knew was when I wrote
frightened from Fort George. Without a doubt
I did not care for anyone. My parents died
when I was here in Canada. Stupefied,
I stared at the letter, and I had no cash
to take me to Lewis. And I cried
alone in this vast country, imagining how
the funeral snaked its way to Aignish,
the coffin shining yellow by that sea
where as a boy I'd swum. It cannot be
that God is not beside us as we roam.
Iain, you must remember it and in a poem
write it.'

The radio burbled on.
'Smart fellow that. There's not a single question
he cannot answer.'

And the advertisements
lavished themselves on air; the shirts, the pants,
the furniture, the flowers.

His wife's red rose
glowed in the garden, and his long green hose
snaked loopily around it.

                                      'Mary loved this land.
She was an orphan. Never knew her folks.'
He paused a moment. 'You give up these smokes.'
I inhaled my Marlborough in that castleless place,
unfabled, unhistoric, sun-embraced.
The moon was rising far as the Yukon
where the prospectors ghosted and the bears
ambled among the fruit trees, fierce and squat.
Canada was a new monotonous flat,
noiseless, mechanical. So many dead,
starved or alcoholic, ill, in despair,
tramps of the Depression when their bare
hands cradled the soup bowls.

                                And along the sands
of the dirty-shored Pacific obese men
played baseball with their sons, to summon back
the shades of spring, now heavy and opaque.
Fertile manoeuvres of the new quarter-back!

9

Sunday, before the church where the woman preached
I paused in a continual storm of cars
and saw a green snail feeding on a black.
There was an ooze like soot. The spire burned back
into the glitter of a thoughtless sky.
The green snail munched with luscious delicacy
as the cars sped south to new America.
I nearly stamped but didn't. I stared long
at that calm ballet of the black and green.
That leisurely Sunday feast, quiet and serene.
The elders of the island, commissars
(this is our star, our ruinous precious star)
heavy and thickset, sipped the fragrant wine
at the Communion, calm and serpentine.
The snail was eaten and a black ooze flowed
past my wet shoe. And not a single cloud
troubled the just harmony of the skies.
I walked away. Yes, let the black snail die
in the fresh green innocence of Canada.

10

I've watched them on the island sit and shake.
'Another heart attack, another stroke.'
The blue crab nibbles. And the Bible is
their stony book and grave hypothesis
of Adam and of Christ, the one who fell,
the one who rose. The church's bell,
helmet of war and grief, sways to and fro
in the salty air of morning. 'John will know
the peace of angels.' All is coffin-talk.
No novels here, only the holy book,
and the theatre of minister and of fire,
the spirit filling him, the envelope
containing letters, Pauline, anti-Pope,
and the thickset fisherman of Galilee,
in their knitted jerseys. Thank you, Lord, for these
deaths you send to us, children, girls,
young husbands, wives, your own transcendent pearls,
educated towards you, and hell.
Obh, obh, they sigh. This gaunt tremendous mill
fines us like flour, to be your fragrant food,
God of the heavens, insatiate of our blood,
gnawing at daffodils and bodies too.
The worms our violinists, undulating crew.
Saws and good proverbs, we are fish well caught
at evening in your red infuriate net,
burning and burning. Oh our sinful souls!
What are our talents and our gifts and skills
in the laundry of our God? We sit, suspire.
The windows rattle our windows, and the spire
of our plain uncoloured church. The minister's gown
billows in storm, his neck as thick as stone
is beaded with the rain, with merciful dew.
Obh, obh, we mutter, swaying. The to-do
of shattered slates is God's majestic curse.
Cut daffodils are blazing in the hearse
and the gravestones nod together. We are saved.
Spare and new-fashioned, we are God-engraved.
Purged of our vanity and self-regard
the wind howls through us, with God's draughty word.

11

I recalled one night when after leaving Lewis
we stopped in Glasgow in a big hotel.
'I want a bath,' he said. (He stood so tall
white-hatted, huge, by the Enquiry Desk.)
'I'm afraid,' the manager said, 'the water's off.
The plumber's repairing it at this very moment.'
'Did you hear that, Iain? They're Red Indians here.
Sure, the English rule them.' The manager stared.
'Plumbers and ministers, they are all the same.
Lad, you're a Red Indian.' And I shook with shame
till he turned away. And later still that night
sitting in the lounge we saw a group
dressed fit to kill with roses at their breasts
(a wedding party, it was easily seen).
'That woman there, wearing a deep red dress,'
he said as usual in his calm loud voice.
'It reminds me of the colour that we had
in Lewis on the curtains round the bed
in the black house before they built the white.
But everyone here's Red Indian, that's quite right.
When I was growing up you never heard
of Scottish history, but only of the kings
of England and of France. The teacher made
you learn the capitals of foreign lands.
Sure, I was taught all that. We were the slaves
of Empire in those days: and you still are.
What was Paris, London, to a fisher
lad on a drifter sailing in the Minch?
I was a coiler: used to coil the rope
for miles and miles, then give the crew their breakfast.
Sometimes they'd let me steer. Calm as the Pope,
and prouder, on these mornings of low mist
I'd take the wheel, a captain and a boy,
the morning sweet and blue as amethyst.
But you're Red Indians here.

                                                    'I knew a Cree
they'd taught the Gaelic Bible to. Let me see.
One of your kin was married to a squaw.
He was a manager in Hudson Bay,
and learned the Indian languages, wrote a book.

And now you're here like a herring on a hook.
Richard the Lionheart, what was he to me?
I still remember all that poetry
about daffodils and cuckoos and the rest.
I liked these verses. Sure, I'll recite you most
of what we learned in Lewis, like "I must
down to the seas again."

                                         'And there was one
about the Relief of Lucknow, when they heard
the pipes approaching. And I cried and cried
from Campbell vanity and Campbell pride.
Sure, I remember that.'

                                         In the hotel
he orated steadily from his adamant will
while I, Red Indian poet, cowered by
tables laden with white gin and whisky.

12

'I'll tell you how I met my wife,' he said.
'You'd almost call it fated.' And he smiled.
'She was an orphan as I think I told
you earlier on. She was a maid in London,
but originally from the area of Loch Lomond.
She's seen a poster showing California
and thought she'd emigrate, owning nothing here.
One day however she saw another poster,
this time of BC, and changed her mind.
She'd go to British Columbia instead.
Similarly I was going to Australia
with a mate of mine from Lewis who fell ill.
I changed my mind and sailed to Canada.
And so one night at a ceilidh and a dance
neither of us knowing in advance
how the other changed his mind, we met. I knew
at the first glance she was the girl for me.
She was standing at the door, nervous and shy,
in Vancouver while a friend of mine from Ness
played the accordion. What do you think of that?'

And he smiled largely. 'When I was home I sought
all round the Trossachs where her home had been
but never found it. She left at seventeen
to go to London, earn her livelihood,
as a maid in service.'

                       'Tell you what,' he said,
'the violin is my favourite instrument,
only I couldn't play it. I played the pipes.
Sometimes on a Saturday we would fish
in the big lakes. And then she'd say, Please stop
(I drove like the furies then). And then I'd go back.
She'd seen a flower she wanted.'

            Like a rock
he sat in the fading light, his wife now dead.
No flowers would grow around that bare bald head.

13

Surrounded by widows like a tribal chief
he'd say, 'The men are dying here like flies.
Insurance, real estate, they never last.
These widows sell their houses and buy flats.'
He'd give them cherries and they'd bake him scones.
'Sure I know you, Dorothy, from a child.'
And then they'd say, 'That Torquil, he's so wild.'
Outside, the punctual avaricious crows
feasted on the cherries in white light.
The brisk cans jangled round his Stetson hat.
'Where houses are now built I'd shoot wild duck.
The husbands die. They never have much luck.
They offered me thousands of dollars for this house
but I'll not leave it.'

                   And the widows came
laden with scones and cakes. 'There's one from Ness,
her son-in-law is ambassador to Moscow.
She still makes oatcakes. Her grandchildren's room
has record player, billiards, and TV.
Imagine that. I saw a millionaire

walk dripping through her house straight from the sea
in nothing but a towel. He said, Hi,
leaving behind him a damp trail of prints.
Just like anyone else he was. Like Smith's
apes he had black hair across his chest!
They hold big parties and they make their deals
in real estate by moonlight on bare heels
squatting around a barbecue like squaws.
The widows rule in Canada. Husbands drop
dead of heart attacks, sometimes at the wheels
of their Cadillacs big as cruisers.'

                                                           He peels

an orange or an apple in a flare
of snaky skin.

                                       'If this was Paradise
Eve would be widowed, Adam would be dead
of a heart attack in Eden's luscious red,
always attracted by another ad.'

14

From superficial Canada I saw
the white ship swelling with her ruinous sails.
The emigrants are dressed in their new suits.
Handkerchiefs wave from the pier and from the boats.
Someone begins a psalm, and the music floats
eerily between the Atlantic and the shore.
Someone is slamming a big salty door.
From salt-scaled pier the scales rise, sharp and pure.
This is their drama and their literature.
The island's bare but for the few sparse trees
around the Castle. There's a cold sharp breeze
drifts between the mother and the son.
To him it's an adventure, to her, ruin.
The ship begins to move. The voices fade.
Sometimes by masts at moonlight they'll hear the dead
voices crying over the wrinkled waves.
The moons are coins gambled from shifting graves,
magnetic eyes that follow them. 'You are the one

I loved more sweetly than my own doomed kin.'
Skid Row awaits them or delusive farms.
Some will return as bankers, some in dreams
recall their crofts by the demented sea.
The steamer's gone. Less than a pin it is.
Its mast slants gravely towards Canada.
The mothers turn away from the milky foam.
The horses in light gigs will steer them home.

15

'You had to watch yourself in Canada.
One day we missed our train (my mate and I)
and both went to a pub. (Pubs keep you warm.)
I woke in a haystack, all my money gone.
(The barman had given me a Mickey Finn)
and found myself in court. I started swearing.
The judge looked over his glasses, said to me:
"I should by all rights send you to prison."
My mate hushed me, pointed to his head,
and told the judge, "The words that he just said
he doesn't understand. He speaks only Gaelic."
The judge remarked, "I'll fine you then instead."
And so he fined me. All that day I searched
for the barman who had given me the drink,
but couldn't find him. I'd have murdered him.
We spent that night inside our hired room,
furniture piled at the door, but no one came.
I'd never been in trouble in my life.
They said I had wrecked the bar before my mate
dragged me out and dumped me on the stack
to sleep my drunken sleep off. It was a town
somewhere in the prairie that it happened.
I remember the first day I saw a waitress
in a hotel where we'd gone to get our breakfast.
There was a menu, (which we'd never seen),
I examined it and saw that there was mush,
much like our porridge. All my pals, too bash-
ful to order breakfast, said I could do it. So
I ordered breakfast. When we were going out
this chap from Stornoway came up and said,

"You shouldn't have ordered ham and egg for me;
you know that I don't like it." And I laughed.
That fellow died in Flanders. When we left
we found a job laying track for the CPR.
Eightsome reels we danced to keep us warm
in the bare box-cars. I remembered autumn
nights in Lewis in the open air,
dancing to the melodeon on the road.
The moon was shining brightly overhead.
I tell you, Iain, these moons were red
and round and heavy. You could hear the boots
thumping till morning on the moonlit road.
And so we danced in the box-cars to keep warm.
It was so cold, so cold. But we were young.
We travelled west till we came to BC.
And then I thought, At last I have come home.
There were hills, the water round Vancouver
reminding me of Lewis, but for the trees.
The flowers were blossoming in Stanley Park.
Lewis was bleak and treeless, and the wind
blew round it in the winter. It was mild
here in the west. I thirsted for the sea,
these days I travelled through the endless prairie.
The ships from other lands lay in the bay,
all black and foreign. Lewis was far away,
a ring in the water that we'd never see.
Why was it we had to leave, I'd say:
the English never left. We were the birds
that like the cuckoo had to cross the sea.
We broke our hearts among these foreign stones.
I sometimes used to imagine Lewis bones
shining in the moonlight and the drunks
swaying from pub to pub: in smelly bunks;
stranded in camp, eating repulsive food.
One day I was with the campers who had queued
for their food in the canteen. Before me stood
an Italian (who had a feather on his collar).
Innocently I put my hand forward
to flick it off, and touched him. And he turned
quick as a flash, a long knife in his hand.
He would have killed me but a chap from Gress
happened to have a hammer, which he raised.

Imagine that! And you couldn't find
a nicer man than that Italian.
Violence burst from everywhere in those days.'
He showed us a film that he had taken in Lewis
with a movie camera that he could hardly use.
Black-skirted women raced past churches. Leaves
seemed to grow at a hundred miles an hour.
'That Gaelic singer now with a guitar
and a Mexican moustache, that goes too far.'
A red plane circled his capacious house
like a bee or wasp, lazy, luxurious.
He had a basement where he used to carve
chairs and tables.

                     There was a pile of old
Scottish magazines. *The Scottish Field,
The Scottish Magazine*.

        And some *Readers Digests*.
'Odd things you'll read there. They have now made tests.
There are pictures of spacemen in the pyramids.'
Craggy, with his carved Red Indian face,
he sat in White Rock in his rocking chair.
I dozed green-capped in that monotonous clear
sunlight that never varied. I missed the dark
enigmas of my Scotland with its stark
bare bloodstained history. The ballads shone
bleakly over restaurant and petrol station,
Anne Hathaway's Cottage, Ye Olde Coffee Shoppe,
the Tartan Gift Shop, and Old English Towne,
the Haunted House, the World of Charles Dickens;
on Fable Cottage with its slanted roof
and swaying gnomes prospecting, and the turf
so brilliant green – replicas of home,
inventions of nostalgia, third-rate poems,
imported and replanted.

                        'I'd not stay
on Lewis now. My mates are in the ground,
there or in Flanders. I used to walk around
the cemeteries, on holidays. I don't know,
I tell you, anyone in Lewis now.

At the airport I would buy a new Maclean –
have you ever read him? *Guns of Navarone?* –
and read it on the plane. I'd read it twice.'
My Proust, my Hardy! These luxurious
morsels snatched from indigence as it flies.
The huts were dirty, beds alive with fleas.
The ghosts cast shirts on spacious summer days,
plunged in the waterfalls.

                                 On a bony chair
I read my Eliot. Under foreign moons
I aimed through yellow teeth at the spittoons.

16

Profound and bitter days. Remember thee,
yes I'll remember thee, thou cheerful ghost
hobbling under the stage with your bad news.
Those diaries of the lost, the lost, the lost!
Yet you come back with brilliant tartan caps
and tartan jackets. 'They left from Glencoe,
my great grandparents in the dizzying snow.'
Hollywood creations in their kilts!
Such colours never shone on sea or land.
Clearing the spruce trees, they found underground
the bones of displaced Indians with their bows.
Alcoholics of the precincts!

                                    Shifting these
even older ghosts they planted their new corn.
In these big acreages they were reborn
painted like pheasants to come back once more
to the cheap gift shops to once indigent shores.
Poor ghosts, poor ghosts! For this new world's a stage
all changed, imperfect. Parrots in a cage
of alien plumage in their tartan shrouds
they are Mackays, Macdonalds and Macleods.
In the middle of their days from Calgary,
the Bronx, Vancouver, seeking to be free
from coronaries, ennui, be reborn
in Uist, Lewis.

                              Burnsians to a man!
The sentiments of colour and of death,
they're stained glass windows on a once plain church.
Red Indians returned! These clouds of froth!

17

The Canadian papers thump through the letter box.
The coloured comics burn.

                              'We had nice socks
our mothers knitted for us. These we sold
to buy new jobs to keep us from the cold.
Once, we left at Easter with our packs
to cross the snow and frost. We had to dump
most of our clothes. We were sinking to our knees
and cut to ribbons by the knives of ice.
Behind us streams of clothes, discarded pants.
We were laying flags of shirts along the trail.
This was in March, sail on sail on sail.'
The weighted papers with their coloured ads!
Sweet cornucopias for big-bellied lads
who once were taut and springy in their pride.
Texan soap operas on the goggle box –
such throwaway riches, treasuries, and flocks
of beautiful iron chicks with brooches, rings,
the shimmering silks, the weightless angel wings.
The vests and pants that stiffened among rocks!

18

The second sight now. 'I will tell you this.
When I was young I used to see this face
gleaming by my bed. I used to dream
of someone ploughing our bare croft in Lewis.
There was a girl strolled round it in white dress.
Whenever I dreamed that dream there was a death.
For instance now, I joined the Fire Brigade,
eventually was Chief. One day in May
we heard the fire bell ringing. So we ran

                              123

and scrambled quickly into the horse wagon,
a converted Oldsmobile. Now all this time
a sheet of glass surrounded me, so dumb
and calm around me the whole wide world seemed.
Lieutenant Mackenzie, Driver Fulton, were
two of the men: the others Bell and Farr.
Struggling into my coat, still caged in glass,
I tried to fit the helmet on my head
while the wagon jolted on, abrupt and fast.
At the junction of 12th Avenue and a street
whose name I now forget (and while my head
inside the railing steadied as I tried
to adjust my helmet) a big fast car sped
towards us and hit us. And I jumped,
told Bell to jump. I woke in hospital.
All except me were violently dead.
Saved by my helmet and my dream I lived.
(We used to find the dead like turkeys, bald
in room on room on room. And once I found
a lady in a chair like a burning throne.
She had no hair: her head was a red moon.)
So always when I had this dream I knew
a death would come. How do you explain this, Iain?
We live, I think, in a country of the unseen.
Some nights I'd wake (a mate in the same room)
to see this lady white and cold and dumb.
"Torquil," he'd shout, "why don't you go to sleep?"
At breakfast they'd laugh.

                                         '"Torquil," they'd say,
"has seen his girl friend. Why doesn't she come by day?"
And so I learned to be silent, being shy.
But often I'd see her and I'd shout and cry.
Explain that if you can.

                                         'No, we don't die.
We meet our wives, I tell you: and our mates.
And Canada was ghostless, blatant, clear.'
I tipped my hat and dozed in the garden chair
while the cherries ripened, and he walked about
restlessly, in his white and dazzling shirt.

19

Widows, wives and husbands in his house
gathered for a ceilidh, and sang songs.
'I love *Loch Lomond*, don't you think it's fine,'
said a fresh-faced woman clad in Campbell tartan.
'Iain doesn't like it,' Torquil said.
'You'd better sing the Gaelic songs instead.'
So someone sang the poem by a bard
who'd come to Canada after his wife had died.
His heart was broken in that land of snow.
'Gold will have its stain, and moss will grow . . .
but love will never die where once it's been . . .'
I saw my uncle's eyes brim with slow tears.
'How many widows, Torquil, do you know?'
someone shouted then.

                                         'Iain believes

Loch Lomond's sentimental.'

                                         All these graves
shining in Canada, that delusive gold,
the ghosts prospecting in the bitter cold.
'We danced in box-cars lest our feet should freeze.'
'Shawbost's most beautiful . . .' 'Kilts show off your knees.'
'Another vodka, whisky . . .'

                                     'From the mast
I saw my village sliding quietly past.'
The Canadian anthem.

                                 'Iain, did you know
someone translated *Jingle Bells*.' 'To Gaelic?' 'No!'
And *Auld Lang Syne* we sang.

                                 In glimmering furs
they drifted round their cars with bag and purse.
The night was huge and calm. The widows burned
with longing, love and grief. Their smart clothes mourned
insurance men, realtors.

                       'O Cuckoo,
please tell me where you've travelled, cold and blue.'
My uncle filled the cherry baskets. They
were half in Canada and half 'at home'.
'Take Iain now, you cannot read a poem
of his and understand it.'

                            To 'yon braes'
the ghost returned in spirit, and the rose
far from Loch Lomond glimmered in the dark.
'Health to the men who sailed through hail and flake
to the land of promise. They'll not feel the cold.
Our potatoes rotted in their greenish mould.
Nothing will grow for us here . . . Health to the men
who sailed to heaven, they'll not come again.'
The fine furs glimmered. And the car doors slammed.

'*Sea Fever* was the poem I preferred,'
my uncle told me.

                    And the night was calm.
'Who are you, uncle?'

                     'And I left that farm
in Manitoba, though the farmer said
"You can have my daughter, my farm, when I am dead."
I packed a case and hitched a lift that night.'
The ring of *Auld Lang Syne* was pure and white.
The widows sleep in meagre beds.

                       The crows
hover above the cherries and the rose.
The tin cans jangle.

                     'I am glad he died,
that brash moustached Major.' And the bride
ghosted above the croft.

                     His craggy face
jutted above glasses.

                     Let my hand
extend from Lewis to this other land,
from Eliot to *Loch Lomond*.

                              Let me speak
of art, of music, where these tall trees
break empty horizons.

                                   Lucid as a bell
Canada twinkles and the sleigh upends.
The pipe is floating on the water.

                         You
turn from the cars, the furs, that greenish shoe.

20

Skid Row and Chinatown. We walked in red.
The drunks were lying limply on the road.
'This is where a lot of fellows died,
broken, alcoholic.' There strolled past
a rouged short-skirted lipsticked prostitute.
I thought of my uncle back in Garrabost
shouldering his scythe in the early morning dew.
It was evening here (eight hours' difference).
He strode through Skid Row with his camera.
Hi, said the drunks, and stretched out trembling hands.
My other uncle was a shade, a ghost.
He'd never been to America; on a plane.
But had fought in Egypt with the Militia.
'He wouldn't come to Canada,' Torquil said.
'I said he could have the croft when my father died.'
The lights were yellow, then the lights were red,
as if we were wounded, covered in our blood,
Culloden of the drunks, the failed, the dead.
My uncle wasn't dead. Largely he strode
about this theatre where men in cloaks
talked to each other, and the whores made trade.
An autumn moon was shining overhead.
'The moon that takes us home to Lewis, the
moon of the barley,' shining on the sea
and painting across it a long luminous road.
We drove away in his long white limousine.
The ruined battlefield no longer seen.
He had escaped and climbed the ladder to

burnt shaken windows and a flagrant blue.
He was the one the tide hadn't covered yet.
He owed fate nothing, was in no one's debt.

21

At the airport we took cases from the boot.
He carried them for us, like a faithful servant,
though we protested. Then he turned away,
quite abruptly, after shaking hands.
We stood and watched him. Then he wasn't there.
'He didn't want to speak lest he should cry.'
Later the plane rose from that new ground
casting large shadows. His large Stetson hat
was a big shadow. This was now his land.
We entered cloud: he'd enter his own house,
empty and voiceless. 'Lord, what a bright sun.'
The rose would glimmer redly in the garden.
So much was changed, so much Canadian.
That year he died in hospital. Three days
it took to kill him. When he died
we were miles away. His house was sold. I heard
he wouldn't take 'no drugs'.

                    I remembered then
leaving him in Glasgow, in the rain,
and looking back. The windows of the hotel
permitted him to see me, not me him.
The planets glittered. Would he go to them?
Would he meet his wife? Who knows? What classic rhyme
can cure us of loneliness, of life, of death?
He was old in that new country.

                    I prefer
to think of him telling stories in his house,
huge, craggy, confident, while that velvet rose
glowed in the garden below squawking crows.